MW01031780

why are
you taking a
picture of that
acorn

kitchen
runner
7 x 11

bedroom
8 x 10

I'm
instagramming
my breakfast

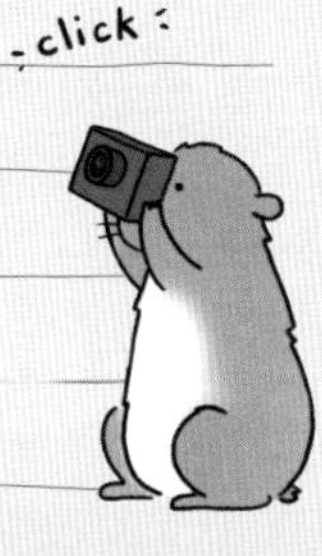
click

we are leaving super early tomorrow, so make sure you set your alarm
okay.

hey tony, wake
me up super
early tomorrow

\

you got
it buddy.

/

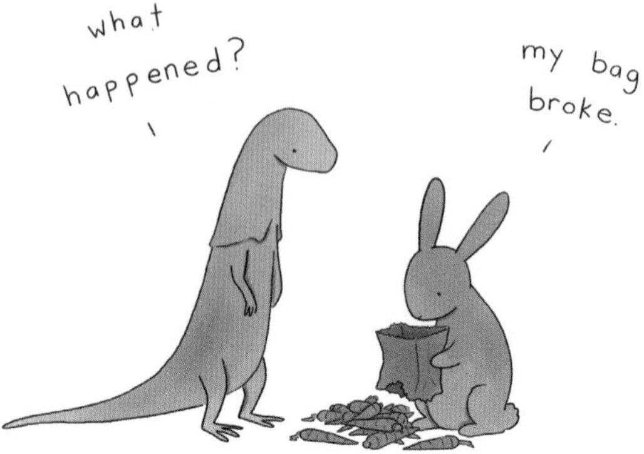
what happened?
my bag broke.

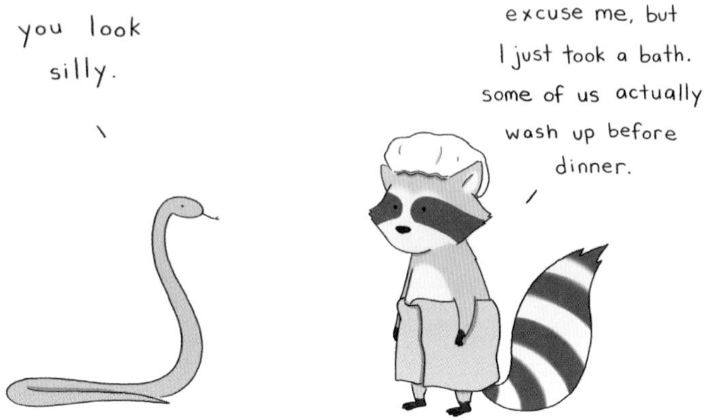
you look silly.
excuse me, but I just took a bath. some of us actually wash up before dinner.

what are
you having?

garbage.

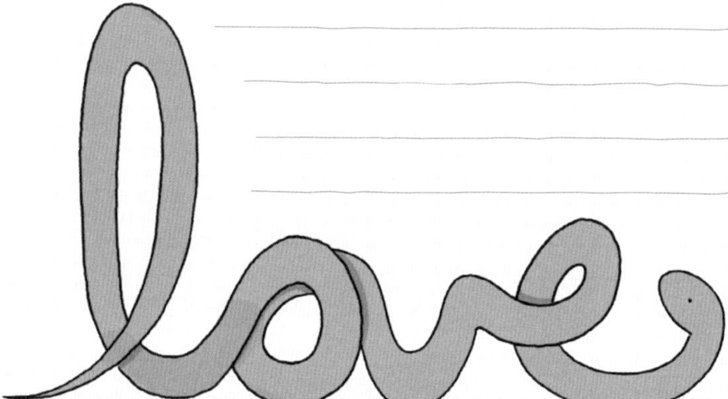
love

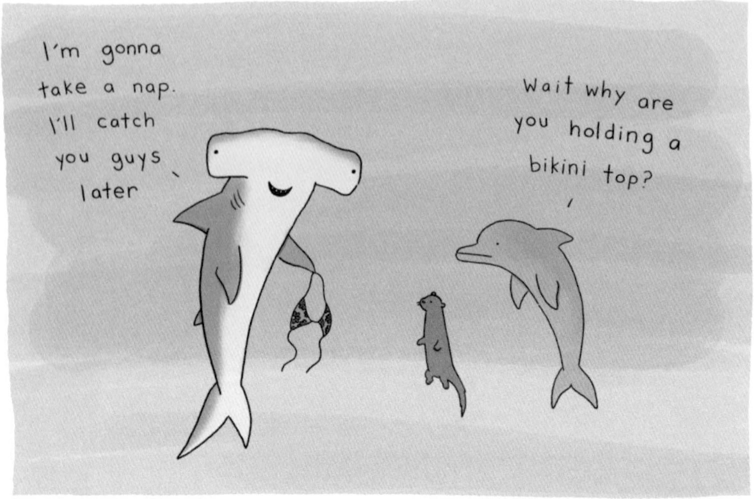
I'm gonna take a nap. I'll catch you guys later
Wait why are you holding a bikini top?

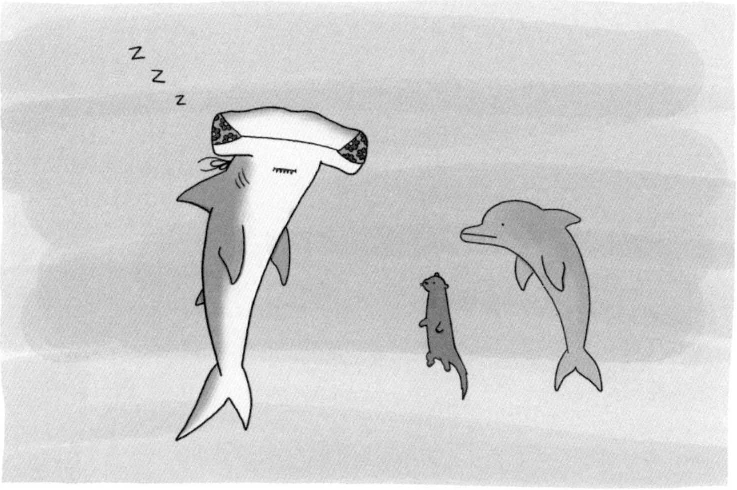
Z Z z

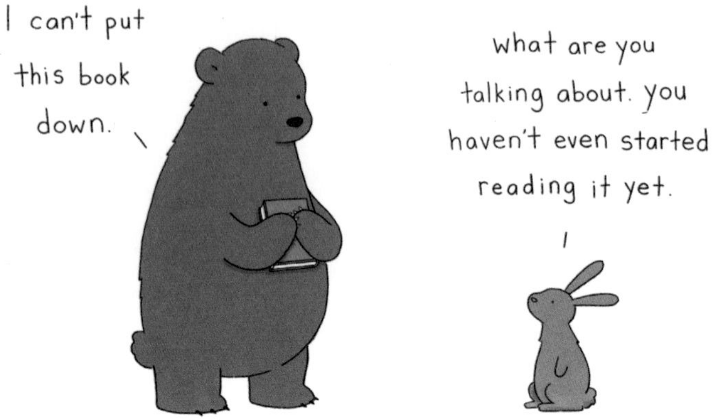
I can't put this book down.
what are you talking about. you haven't even started reading it yet.

no I mean I literally can't put it down. I spilled pancake syrup on it earlier and now it's stuck to my fur.

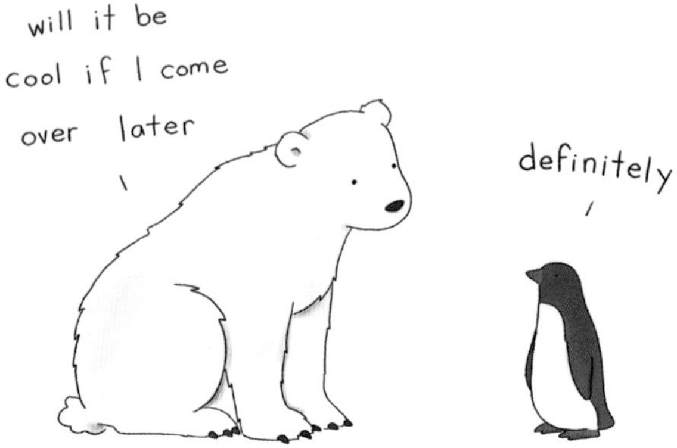
will it be cool if I come over later
definitely

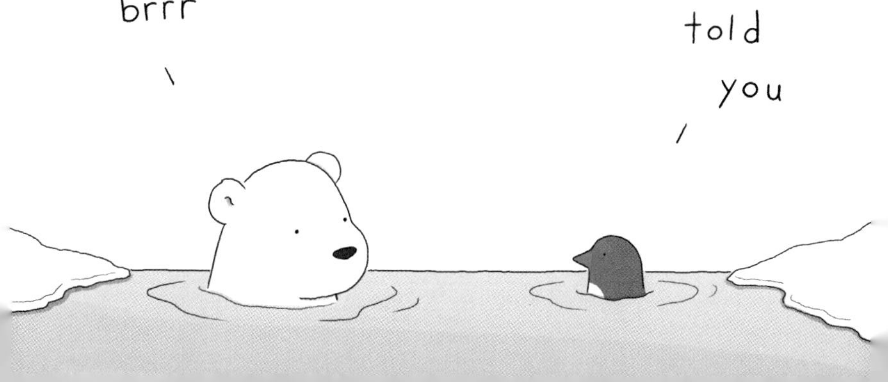
brrr
told you

should we dress up for that party later?
yeah. it's gonna be pretty fancy

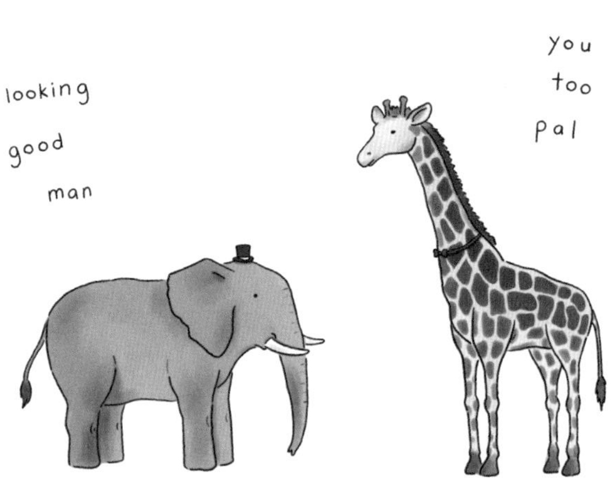
looking good man
you too pal

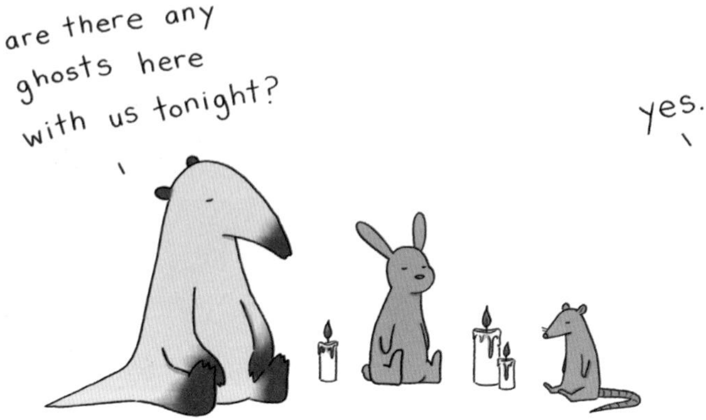
are there any ghosts here with us tonight?
yes.

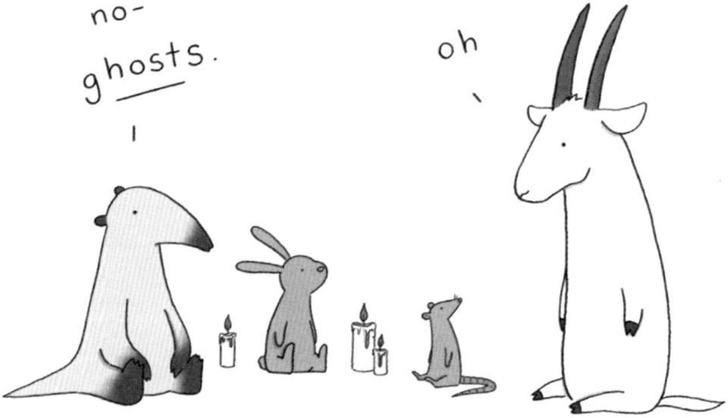
no-
ghosts.
oh

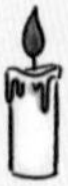
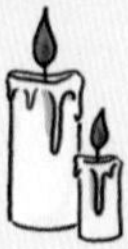

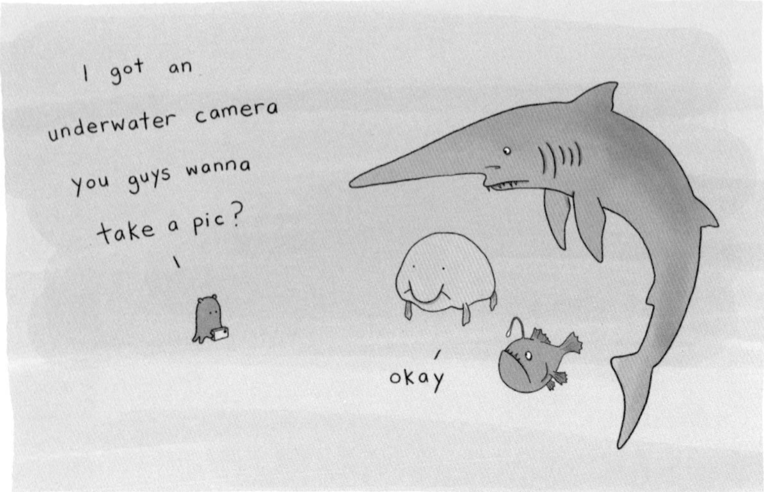
I got an
underwater camera
you guys wanna
take a pic?
okay

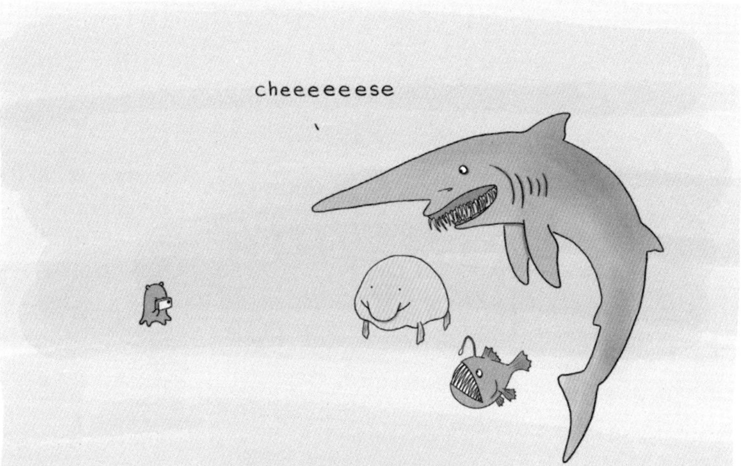
cheeeeeese

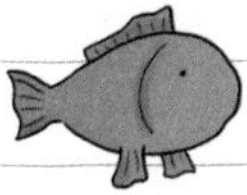
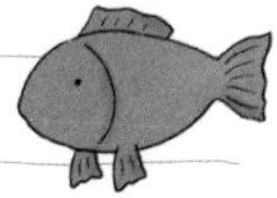

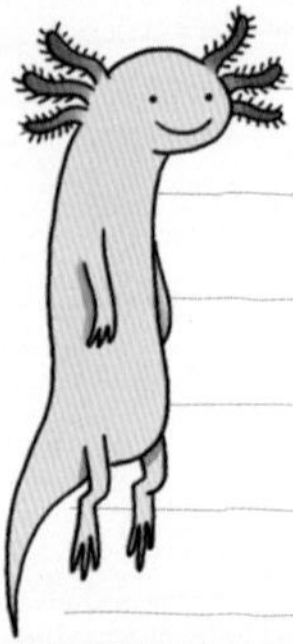

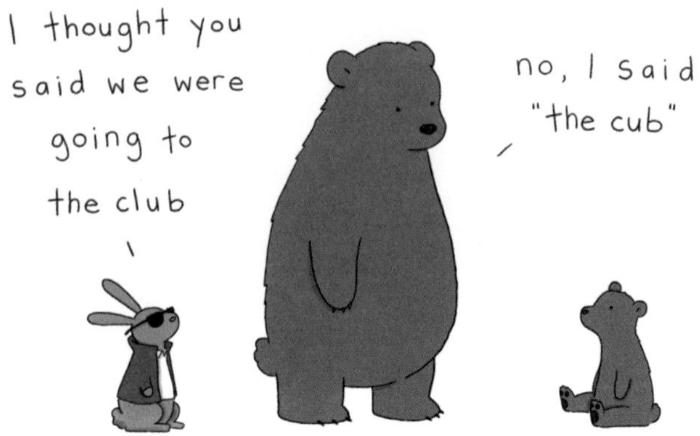
I thought you said we were going to the club
no, I said "the cub"

isn't he
fun?!

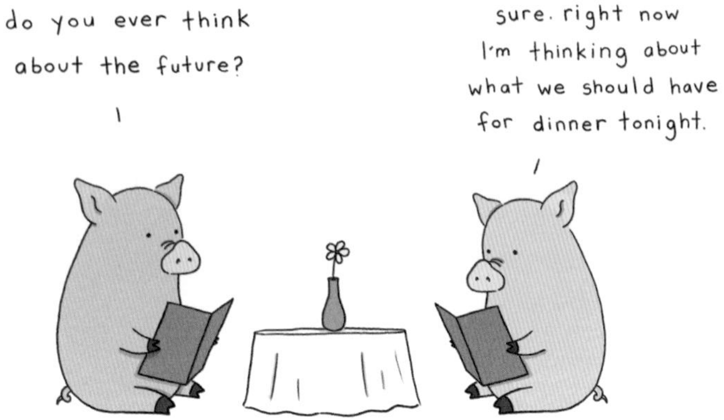
do you ever think about the future?
sure. right now I'm thinking about what we should have for dinner tonight.

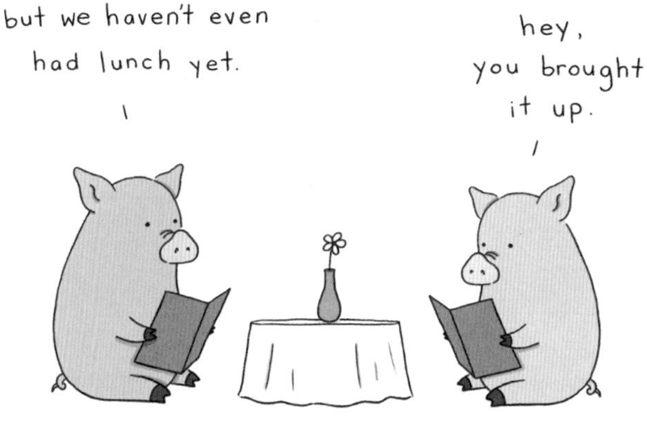
but we haven't even had lunch yet.
hey, you brought it up.

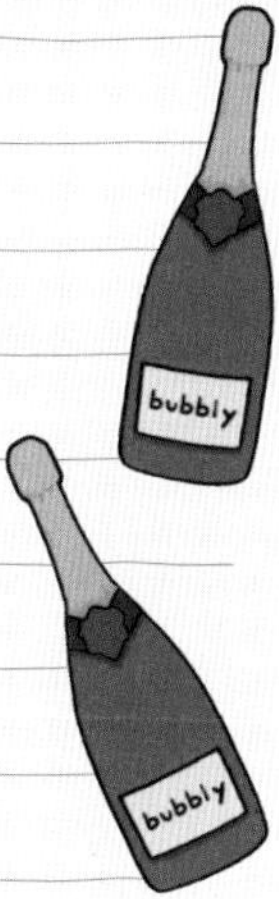
bubbly
bubbly

it's too hot.
my ice cream
is melting

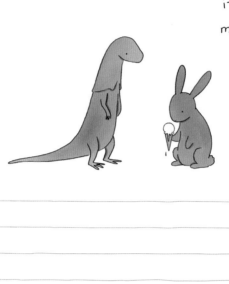

how'd the
job interview
go?

pretty good! I introduced
myself, sniffed his butt,
listed my strengths,
listed my weaknesses...

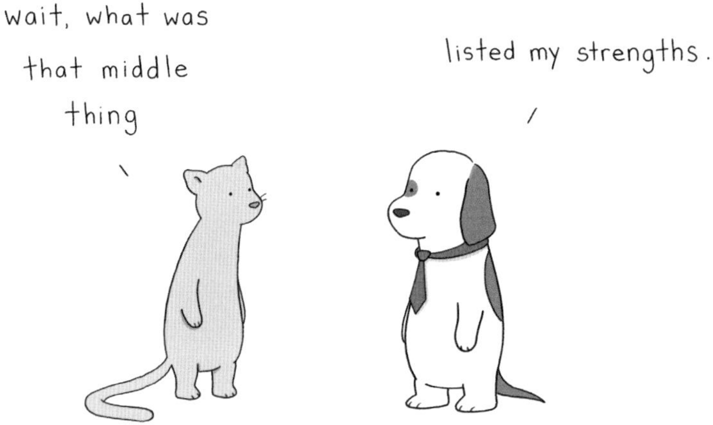
wait, what was that middle thing
listed my strengths.

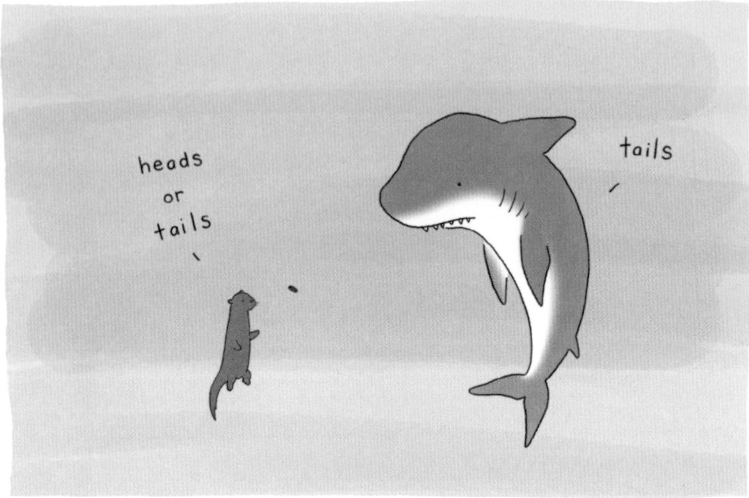
heads
or
tails
tails

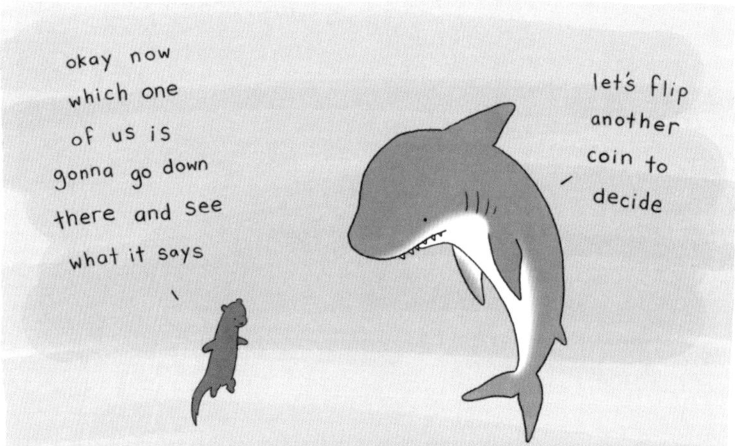
okay now
which one
of us is
gonna go down
there and see
what it says
let's flip
another
coin to
decide

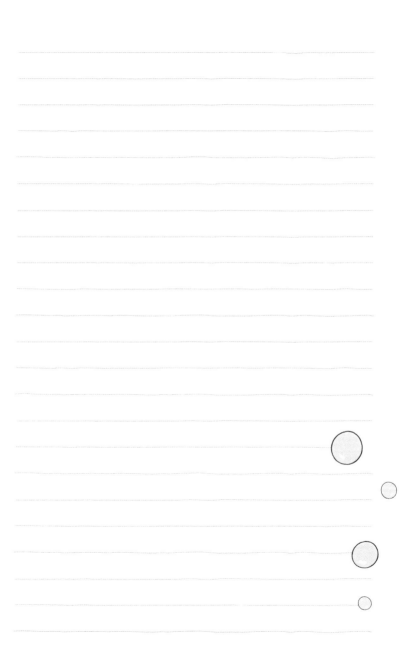

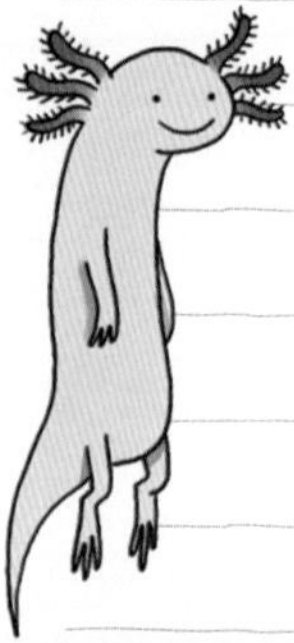

oh is
it snowing
outside?

nah I'm
just eating
a powdered
donut

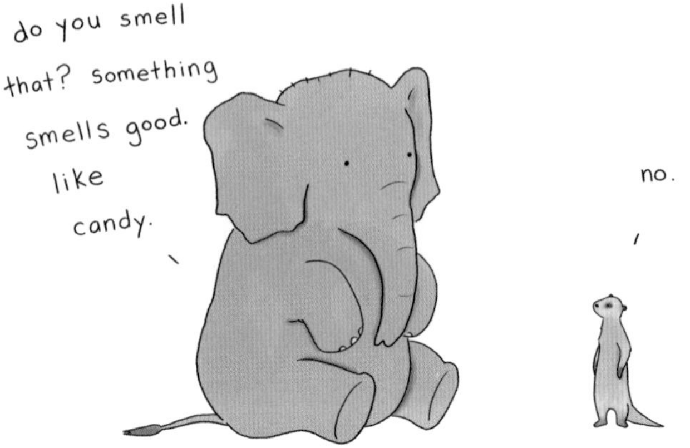
do you smell that? something smells good. like candy.
no.

oh, never
mind. I have
a jelly bean
stuck in
my nose.

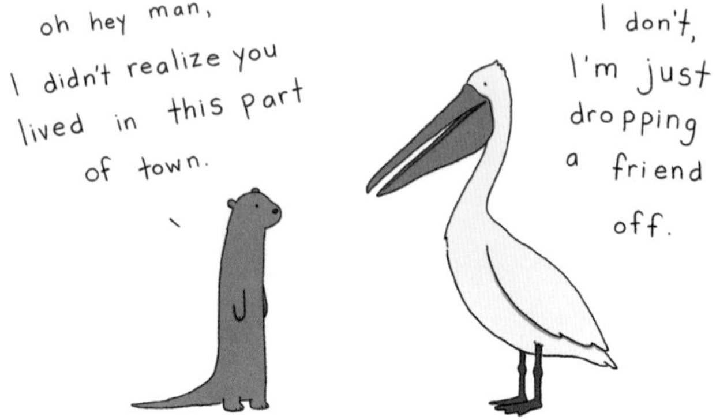
oh hey man, I didn't realize you lived in this part of town.
I don't, I'm just dropping a friend off.

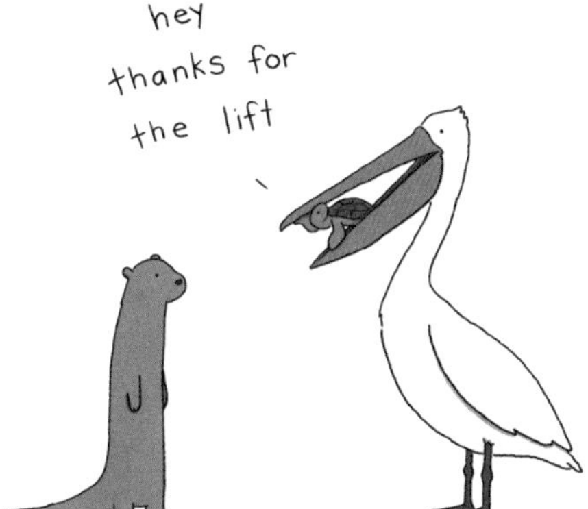
hey thanks for the lift

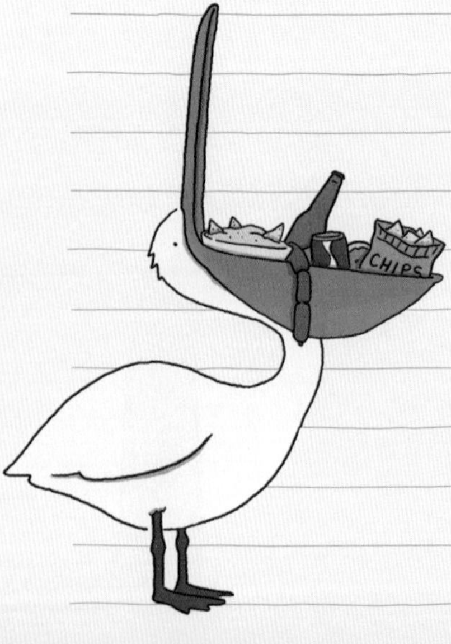
CHIPS

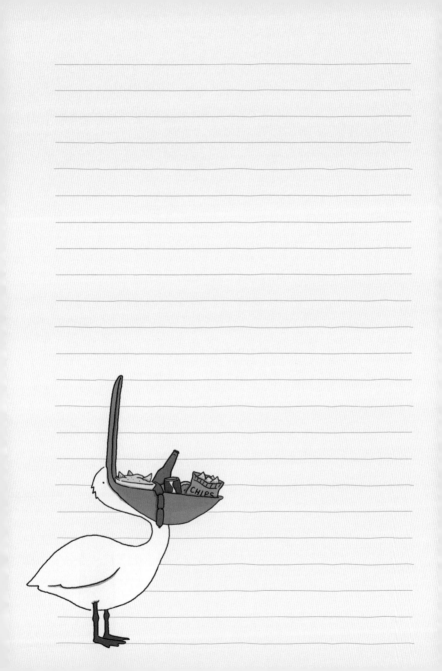

I made a
sand castle!

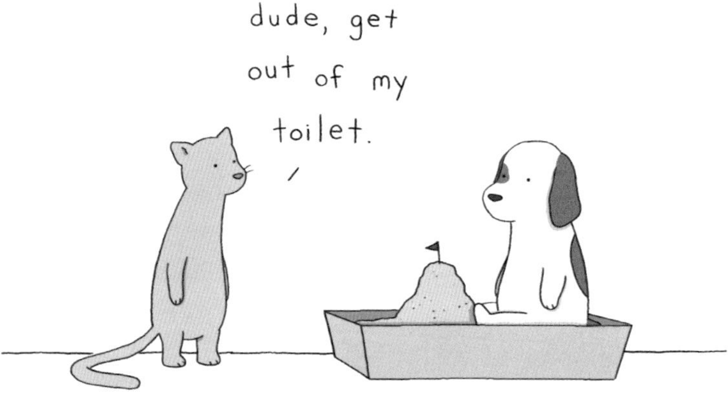
dude, get out of my toilet.

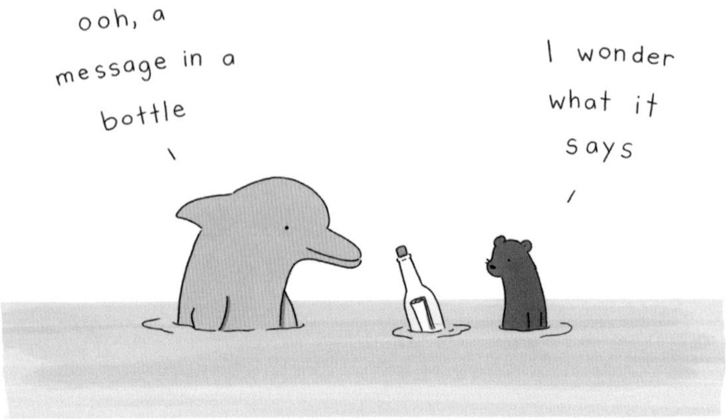
ooh, a
message in a
bottle
I wonder
what it
says

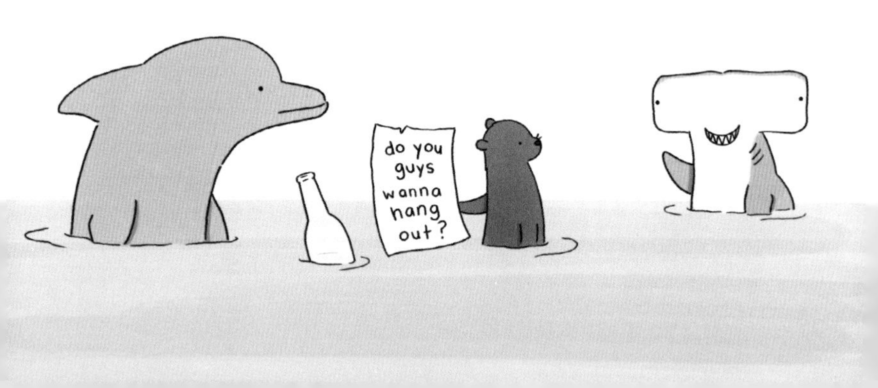
do you guys wanna hang out?

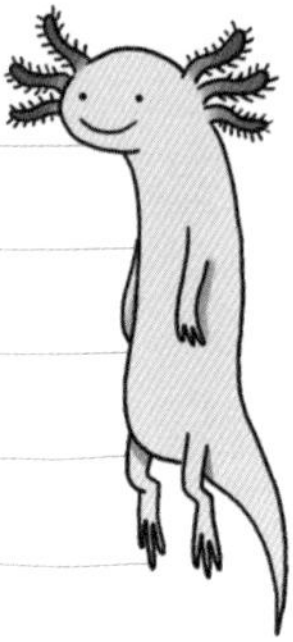

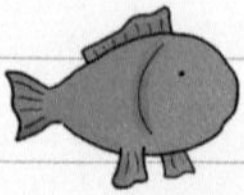

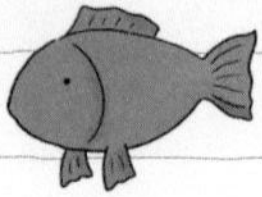

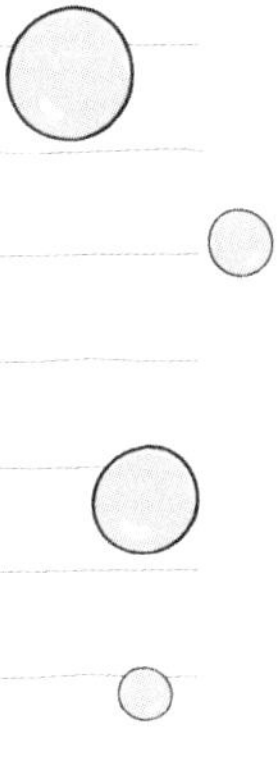

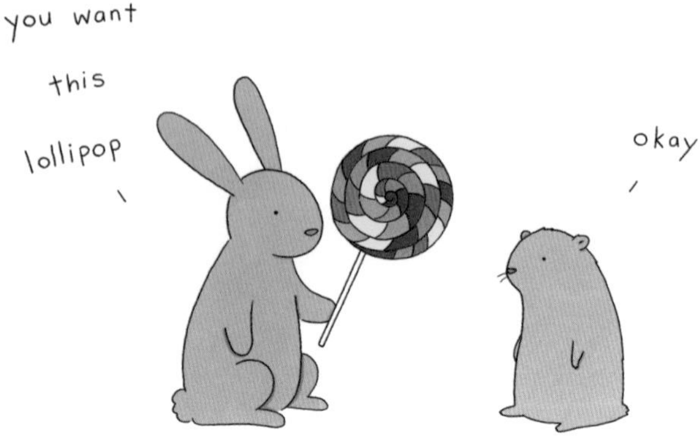
you want
this
lollipop
okay

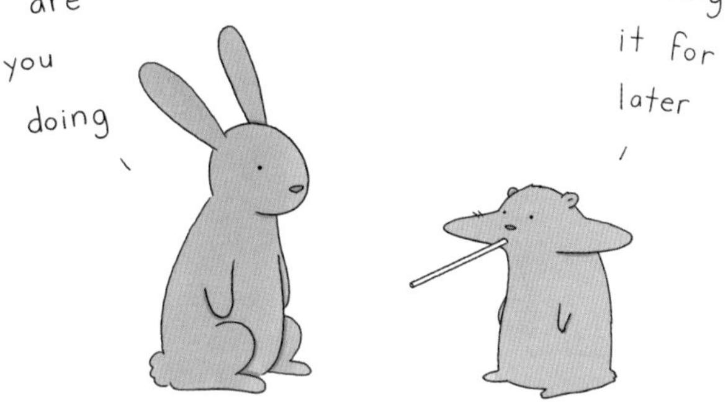
what are you doing
saving it for later

you
just have
to take life
one step
at a time

but I have
so many
feet
/

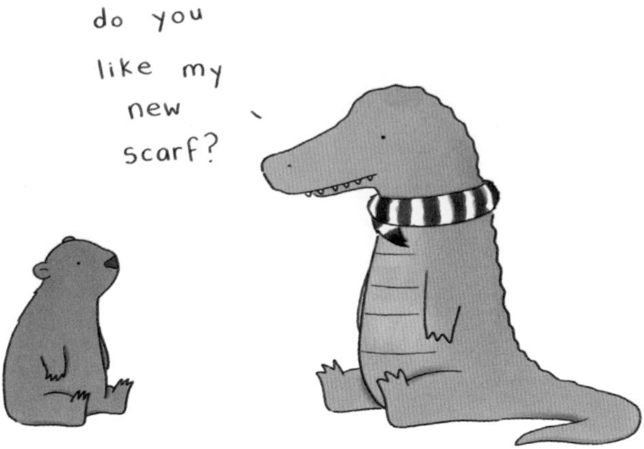
do you like my new scarf?

do
you
mind?

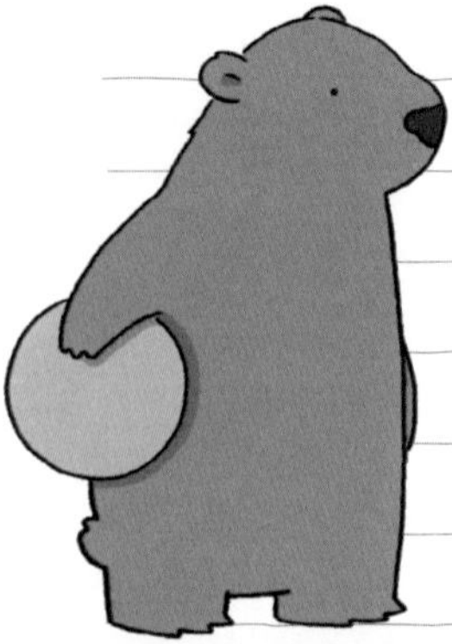

b-e-a-r-s a-r-e
a-w-e-s-o-m-e

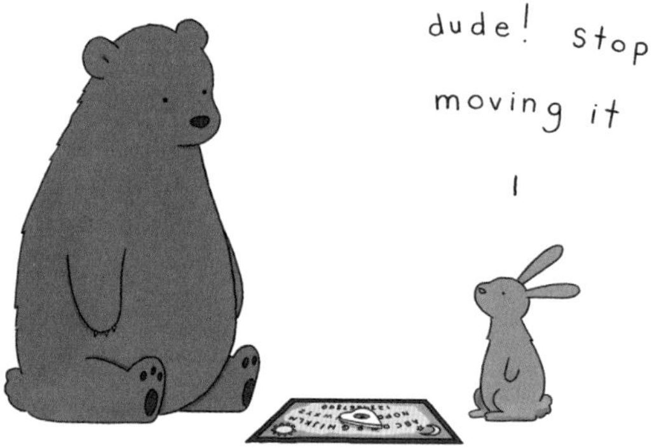
dude! stop
moving it

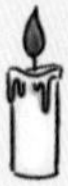 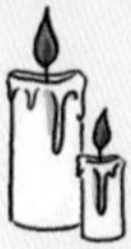

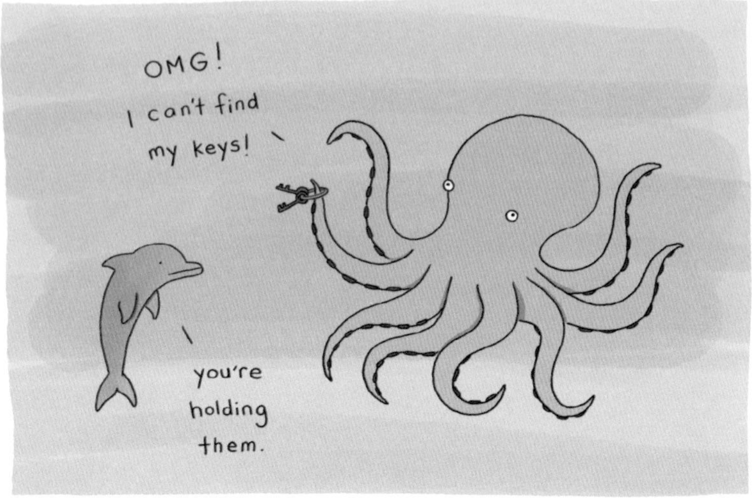
OMG! I can't find my keys!
you're holding them.

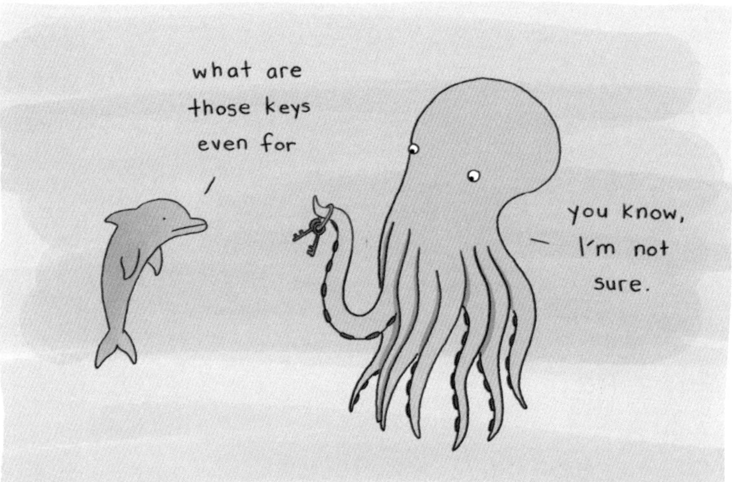
what are those keys even for
you know, I'm not sure.

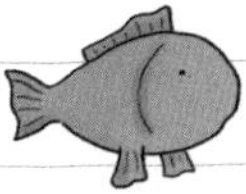
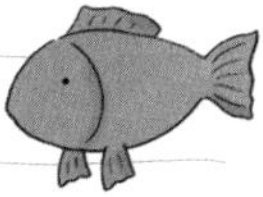

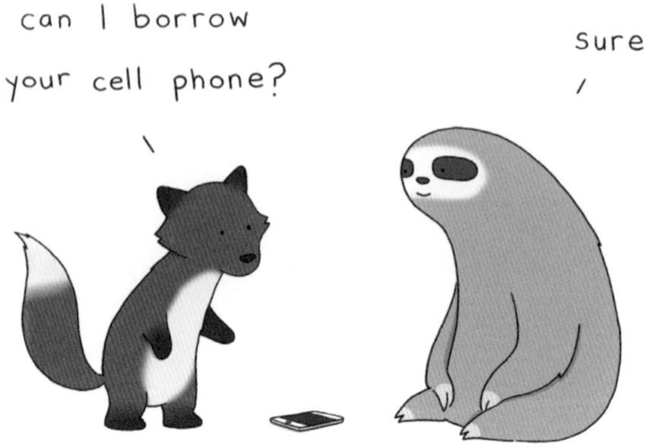
can I borrow
your cell phone?
sure

do you realize
you have 487
missed calls

I can never
answer it in time.

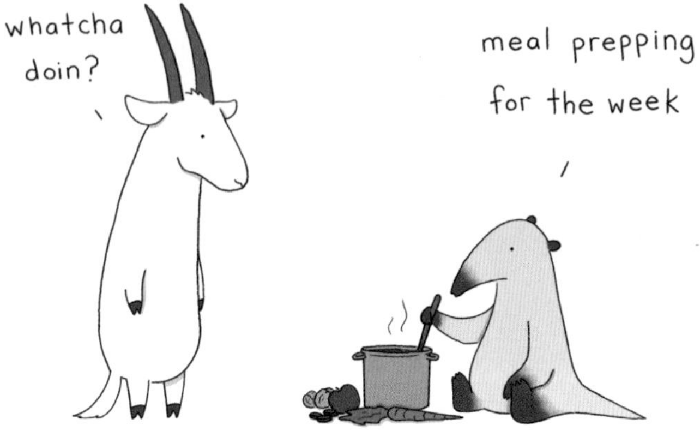
whatcha doin?
meal prepping for the week

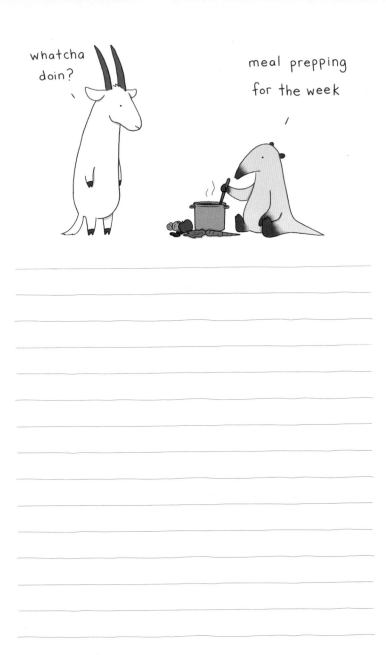

I'm gonna leave this uncovered, and by friday it will be covered with ants.

I caught a fish!
Should we
have him
for dinner?

I hope
you guys
like spaghetti!

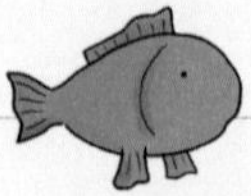

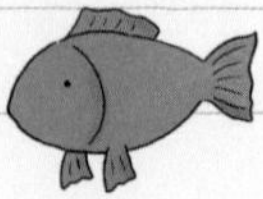

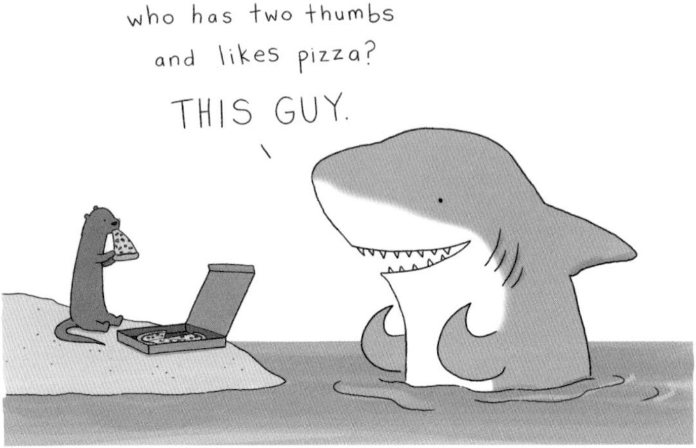
who has two thumbs
and likes pizza?
THIS GUY.

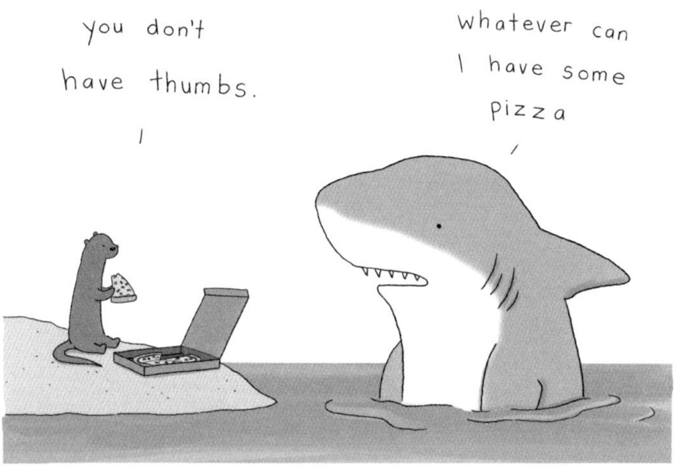
you don't have thumbs.
whatever can I have some pizza

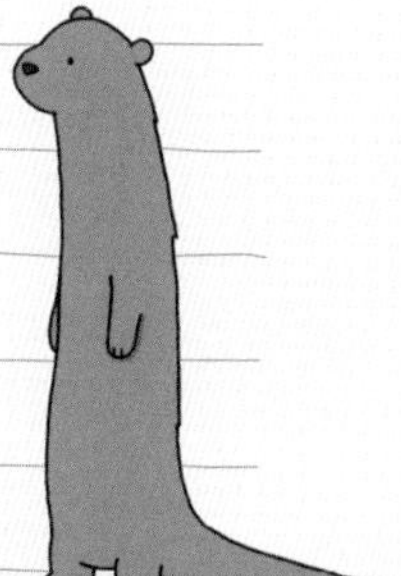

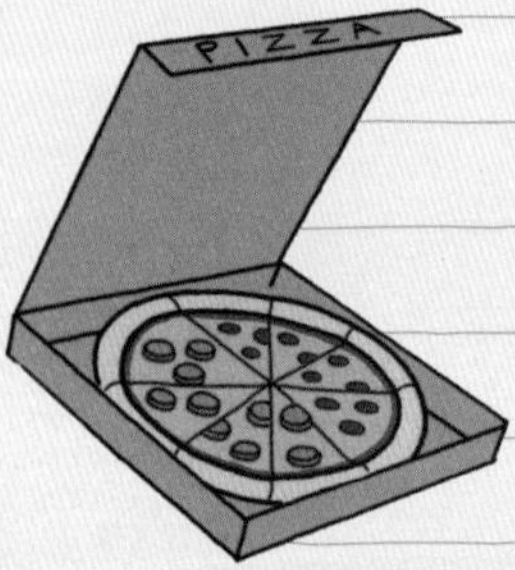
PIZZA

for the last time!
wake up, you have
to go to school.

dad, you're
yelling at a
pine cone.
/

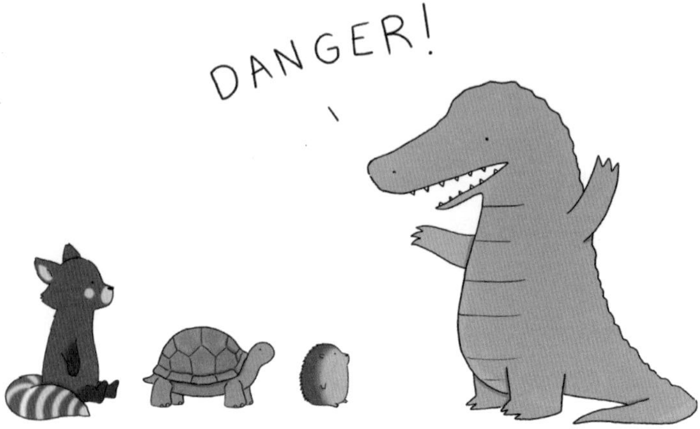
DANGER!

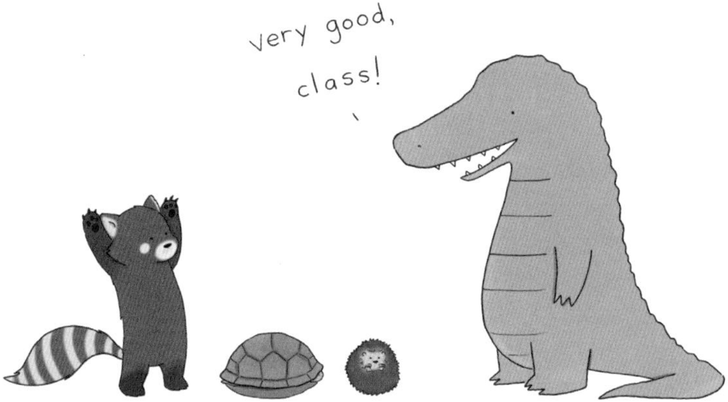
very good,
class!

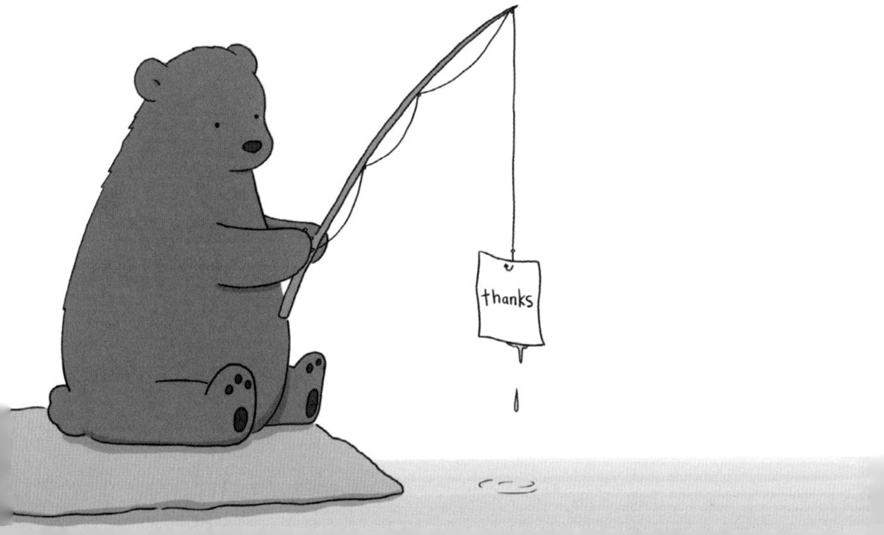
thanks

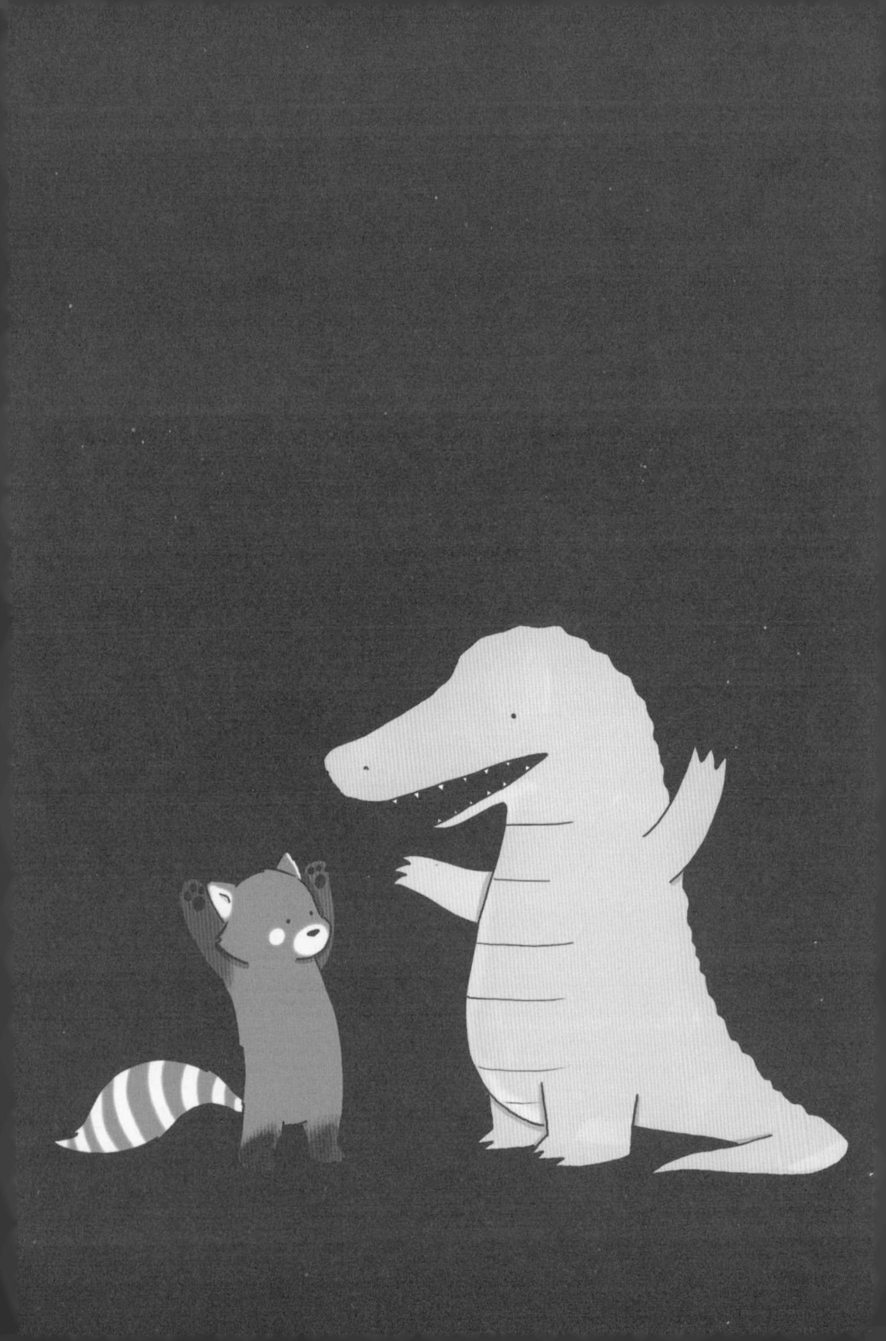